COCA-COLA: ITS VE
IN PHOTOGRAPHS
1930 THROUGH 1969
PHOTO ARCHIVE

Photographs from THE ARCHIVES DEPARTMENT
of THE COCA-COLA COMPANY

Howard L. Applegate

Iconografix

Photo Archive Series

Iconografix
1830A Hanley Road
Hudson, Wisconsin 54016 USA

Library of Congress Card Number 95-82101

ISBN 1-882256-47-6

Reprinted November 2012

Cover design by Lou Gordon, Osceola, Wisconsin

Digital imaging by Pixelperfect, Madison, Wisconsin

Printed in the United States of America

PREFACE

Histories are contained in the books, journals, correspondence and personal papers stored in libraries and archives throughout the world. Written in tens of languages, covering thousands of subjects, the stories are recorded in millions of words.

Words are powerful. Yet, the impact of a single image, a photograph or an illustration, often relates more than dozens of pages of text. Fortunately, many of the libraries and archives that house the words also preserve the images.

In the **Photo Archive Series,** Iconografix reproduces photographs and illustrations selected from public and private collections. The images are chosen to tell a story—to capture the character of their subject. Reproduced as found, they are accompanied by the captions made available by the archive.

A 1930 White Model 61 tractor-trailer.

INTRODUCTION

Coca-Cola is a singular, successful, and ubiquitous American institution. The product and the unique script that identifies it are famous throughout the world. Memorabilia associated with Coca-Cola are the most widely and fiercely collected corporate-devised materials in the world.

Readers with a particular interest in vehicles used by THE COCA-COLA COMPANY and its bottlers will find this book fascinating. The photographs, for the most part, are from THE ARCHIVES DEPARTMENT of THE COCA-COLA COMPANY. To present a more comprehensive history of these vehicles, the author has included certain photographs from his private collection.

Pharmacist, patent medicine and beverage innovator John S. Pemberton reached the zenith of his career in 1886. He produced a new soft drink created from a flavored syrup mixed with soda water and ice. His assistant, Frank Robinson, named it Coca-Cola. Robinson also produced the Spencerian script that became its famous trademark. The first retail sale of Coca-Cola was

recorded May 8, 1886, at Jacobs' Pharmacy in Atlanta, Georgia. It soon became a popular warm weather drink, mixed and served at soda fountains and in train stations, theater lobbies, drug and department stores.

Pemberton died in 1888. By 1891, Asa G. Candler, an Atlanta wholesale druggist, acquired the Coca-Cola secret formula and all rights to its name for $2,300. Candler, a promoter, devoted his energies to marketing Coca-Cola and motivating people to try this custom-mixed drink for themselves. During the next four years, Candler so successfully promoted Coca-Cola that it was in demand everywhere in the United States.

Coca-Cola became popular as a takeout item, but the carbonation rarely survived the trip home. Candler recognized the problem, but held no interest in bottling Coca-Cola for consumption off-premises. By 1899, he sold the rights to bottle and distribute Coca-Cola throughout the United States. The consortium that bought the rights built bottling plants in Chattanooga,

Tennessee and Atlanta. However, it lacked the capital to build a nationwide network. Consequently, it sought others with capital, to whom it granted exclusive territorial franchises and perpetual contracts to bottle and sell Coca-Cola. These entrepreneurs became the backbone of the independent bottler system. Within ten years, independent bottlers built nearly 400 works; by 1925, more than 1,200.

Candler's company and the independent bottlers used contemporary means of transportation to distribute their products. Before 1920, they commonly employed teamsters, who delivered Coca-Cola in wagons drawn by teams of horses or mules. Some bottlers bought the new motor trucks, as experiments. The reliability of motor trucks used by the American Expeditionary Forces of World War I fostered a substantial commercial demand for trucks. Following the war, most independent bottlers were quick to convert from animal power to motor power.

Most early bottle trucks were medium to heavy-duty units. Although some bottlers operated stake trucks, others bought conventional cab and chassis units. Bottlers had their employees, or local woodworkers or blacksmiths, build special bodies with beds that tilted toward a horizontal center wall. Such a design tended to hold cases in place and minimized spillage.

Prior to the 1930s, THE COCA-COLA COMPANY imposed no standards for motor trucks, except for regulations on the use of the Coca-Cola script. In 1923, when Robert W. Woodruff became president, the company began to purchase its trucks from the White Motor Company. Woodruff, who also served as president of White from 1922 through 1924, undoubtedly influenced the choice. Woodruff encouraged the independent bottlers to buy

White trucks, but such a decision was theirs to make. Bottlers bought trucks from a number of companies that included Autocar, Federal, Ford, International, Kelly, Mack, Mitchell, Packard, Rapid, and Stewart. Not only were the independents free to choose their trucks, but also the colors that the trucks were painted. Most selected dark colors. Popular choices included maroon, dark blue, dark green, dark brown, and various shades of gray.

In the mid and late 1920s, many of the panel trucks and tractor-trailers operated by THE COCA-COLA COMPANY were painted with a billboard-type of commercial art that promoted drinking Coca-Cola. Artists painted these mobile advertisements with oil-based paint in a multiplicity of colors. Sometimes, no two trucks in the fleet were alike. As beautiful as these trucks were, Woodruff was concerned with their lack of visual standardization. In the marketing of Coca-Cola, Woodruff believed in absolute standards. Accordingly, in the late 1920s, he adopted bright yellow as the standard color for the company's trucks. Striping, lettering, the undercarriage, and wheel discs were painted red. The company called this "the standard truck painting design." A bottlers' committee on standardization also endorsed the new paint scheme, but their recommendations were not compulsory. Many, if not most bottlers, followed the new standards. Some bottlers, however, did not. Consequently, some trucks in the 1930s and 1940s were painted black, maroon, or gray.

Beginning in the late 1920s, the bodies fitted to bottle trucks became more sophisticated. Each region of the country had at least one, if not several, body companies that deluged bottlers with claims that their products were state of the art. Known as the bottlers rack, these purpose-built bodies were widely adopted. Many of the trucks in this period were fitted with cab advertising boards. These fancy, small signs were attached to the cab roof and featured a current marketing slogan. Similar signs were often carried above the body, as well. Through the 1930s, the fleet of trucks operated by THE COCA-COLA COMPANY continued to be dominated by White. The independents, however, preferred trucks built by Mack, International, Studebaker, Dodge, Ford, Chevrolet, and GMC. Their selection depended on many variables that included price and local dealer support. In certain markets, strong dealer networks influenced their choice of manufacturer. Thus, Studebaker sold well in Indiana; Diamond T and Federal in Illinois. All the truck manufacturers cooperated with the builders of bottlers racks, as they developed new cab and chassis units. The result was an improved and more modern delivery truck.

The color red was, of course, closely associated with Coca-Cola. In the 1950s, the only places yellow dominated was in its application to wooden six packs, cases, and trucks. Yellow continued as the standard color for trucks until about 1957, when The Standardization Committee of the Bottlers of Coca-Cola recommended a new paint design. The three-tone scheme included traditional yellow on the lower portion, with a band of "Coca-Cola" red separating the yellow from the white upper portion. The design appears to have been either a compromise between supporters of yellow and promoters of red, or an intentional choice in the transition to predominantly red trucks, which appeared in 1969.

The photos in **Coca-Cola: Its Vehicles in Photographs 1930 through 1969 Photo Archive** characterize a significant 40 year period in the history of THE COCA-COLA COMPANY. Most are hitherto unpublished. I invite the reader to enjoy the photographs, as they reveal the variety of commercial vehicles and passenger cars that once served THE COCA-COLA COMPANY and its independent bottlers.

I am indebted to the professionals in THE ARCHIVES DEPARTMENT of THE COCA-COLA COMPANY, especially Philip F. Mooney, department manager, Joanne Newman-Johnson, and Brookie Keener. Ron Peck, a noted collector and dealer in materials related to THE COCA-COLA COMPANY, assisted in the identification of photographs. In some cases, it was not possible to precisely date or identify the vehicles or the locations in which they were photographed. So that future editions may be revised to include such details, readers with more definitive information are encouraged to write the author at Box 260, Annville, Pennsylvania 17003 USA. Most of the information about THE COCA-COLA COMPANY and its independent bottlers is from data in THE ARCHIVES DEPARTMENT or from company publications, particularly Anne Hoy's **Coca-Cola: The First Hundred Years**, Revised Edition, 1990.

A 1930 International Model A-5 in front of an unknown bottling plant.

A 1930 White upon delivery to the Pittsburgh, Pennsylvania bottler.

A 1931 Ford Model AA operated by the Birmingham, Alabama bottler.

A 1931 Ford Model AA stake truck used by an unknown bottler for advertising.

A 1931 Ford Model AA 1-1/2-ton panel truck, with advertising on sunshield, on a Denver, Colorado street.

A 1931 American Austin business coupe used for special deliveries by an unknown bottler.

A 1931 Studebaker at an unknown Indiana location.

The El Paso, Texas bottler's 1931 Ford Model AA panel delivery used by servicemen of the advertising department.

A 1931 White Model 641 parked in Long Island City, New York.

A 1930's fleet of White trucks upon delivery to the Greensboro, North Carolina bottler.

A 1932 Ford Model BB parked in Center, Texas.

A 1932 White Model 61 operated by the Coca-Cola Bottling Works, Bethlehem, Pennsylvania.

A 1932 White Model 61 with cab advertising board.

A 1933 Indiana Model 85.

A 1933 White Model 62 with cab advertising board.

A 1933 White Model 62 during a delivery to a ship.

A 1933 International Model A-5 in front of the Spirit Lake, Iowa bottling plant.

Fleet of 1933 Dodge half-ton commercial panel trucks operated by the Terre Haute, Indiana bottler.

A 1933 International Model A-60 tractor-trailer hauling Five-O and Coca-Cola cases.

A 1933 Studebaker and its driver in front of an unknown bottling works.

Fleet of Chevrolet trucks photographed at the Corpus Christi, Texas bottler in 1934.

A 1934 White, with cab advertising board, operated by the Cincinnati, Ohio bottler.

Truck fleet photographed at El Paso, Texas in 1934.

An interesting tractor-trailer photographed on a Memphis, Tennessee street in 1934.

A 1934 White Model 702 operated by the Atlanta Coca-Cola Bottling Company.

A 1934 Mack parked in front of the Charlotte, North Carolina plant.

A 1934 Diamond T Model 405D deluxe streamlined 1-1/2-ton unit owned by the Waterloo, Iowa bottler.

A 1934 White, with body by H. McFarlane and Company, Chicago, used to distribute samples of Coca-Cola.

A 1935 Ford panel delivery truck used by the Superior Bottling Company.

A 1935 Ford delivery truck during a Richmond, Virginia flood.

Fleet of St. Petersburg, Florida trucks in 1935.

A 1935 Ford truck parked in front of the Lincoln, Nebraska bottling plant.

Home delivery in Springfield, Illinois in 1935.

Fleet operated by the Joplin Coca-Cola Bottling Company, photographed on July 14, 1935.

Fleet of 1935 Chevrolet trucks operated by the Vernon Coca-Cola Bottling Company, Vernon, Texas.

A 1935 Ford Model BB parked inside an unknown bottler's warehouse.

A mid-1930's Dodge owned by the Michigan City, Indiana bottler.

A 1936 International Model D300 at an Ohio bottling plant.

A 1936 Diamond T parked in front of the Utica, New York bottling works.

A 1936 photograph of the fleet of Ford trucks used by the Bellingham, Washington bottler.

A 1936 Studebaker delivered to the Reading, Pennsylvania bottler.

A 1936 International Model C-60 long wheelbase truck in Jackson, Mississippi.

A 1936 GMC operated by the Dayton, Ohio Bottling Company.

A 1937 White streamlined, custom-built tractor-trailer at the Birmingham, Alabama location.

A 1937 GMC inside the San Antonio, Texas bottler's warehouse.

A 1937 Mack Jr. Model 21M with cab advertising board.

A 1937 International Model D300 delivering to a tavern.

A 1937 International Model D300 at a Chicago loading dock.

A 1937 Studebaker Model J15. Note the rear compartment for posters, literature, and signs.

A 1938 Ford during a delivery to a Georgia restaurant.

Fleet of Chevrolet trucks and one Ford, photographed at Bangor, Maine in 1938.

Fleet of Ford trucks operated by the Douglas, Arizona bottler, photographed in 1938.

A 1938 photograph of a Chevrolet tractor-trailer in front of the Carlsbad, New Mexico bottler.

A 1938 White tractor-trailer at an unknown location.

A 1938 photograph of the Waco, Texas bottler's truck repair shop.

Delivery of Coca-Cola to New York City subway vending machines, photographed in the late 1930s.

A 1938 GMC cab-over-engine (C.O.E.) at an unknown location in New York.

A 1938 GMC C.O.E. used by the advertising department of an unknown bottler.

A streamlined 1938 International Model DS 300 exiting the Los Angeles bottling plant. Note the white wall tires.

A 1938 Studebaker C.O.E. Model K20M at an unknown location.

A 1938 White C.O.E. Model 802 parked in front of a pharmacy.

A 1939 Studebaker Champion driven by a salesman of an Oregon Coca-Cola bottler.

A 1939 Mack parked in front of an unknown Pennsylvania Mack dealership.

A 1940 Mack Model EHU with cab advertising board.

A 1940 Dodge in front of an unknown bottling plant.

Photographs of the truck fleet, mostly White, operated by the Atlanta Coca-Cola Bottling Company in 1940.

A 1941 photograph of a Chevrolet truck in New York City.

A 1941 International Model K-5, with Hobbs bottler's rack, in San Antonio, Texas.

A pair of 1941 Ford C.O.E. trucks with cab advertising boards.

A 1941 Studebaker Model M16 in front of an unknown Indiana bottler.

A 1941 Chevrolet C.O.E. with cab advertising board.

A 1941 Ford C.O.E. unit with cab advertising board, owned by the Atlanta Coca-Cola Bottling Company.

A 1941 Studebaker Champion salesman's car at a Georgia location.

A 1946 Chevrolet pickup on the streets of Clifton Forge, Virginia.

A 1947 International Model KB-8, with cab advertising board, on the grounds of the Atlanta bottling plant.

Two 1948 Chevrolet trucks operated by the Cleveland, Tennessee bottler.

A 1948 International Model KB-8 inside a Fresno, California warehouse.

Fleet of 1948 Dodge trucks operated by the Coca-Cola Bottling Company of New York.

A 1949 photograph of a portion of the trucks in the Atlanta bottling company fleet.

A 1949 International Model KB-8 on a Fresno, California street.

A 1949 GMC, with Hobbs bottler's rack, ready for delivery to the San Antonio Coca-Cola Bottling Company.

A 1949 Ford Model F100 pickup being painted in the Atlanta body shop.

A 1949 Chevrolet upon delivery to the Harrisburg, Illinois bottler.

A 1949 Ford C.O.E. Model F5 in front of the San Antonio, Texas bottling plant.

A 1949 Studebaker Model 2R16 at an unknown location.

A 1949 Dodge, with cab advertising board, operated by the Anderson, South Carolina bottler.

A 1950 International C.O.E. Model LC-160 at an unknown California location.

A 1950 White Model 3016 ready for delivery.

A 1950 White Model 3022T tractor-trailer owned by the Clarksburg, West Virginia bottler.

A 1950 White tractor with trailer operated by a contract owner.

A 1950 Chevrolet operated by the St. Louis bottling company.

A 1950 International Model L160 with cab advertising board

A 1950 Chevrolet advertising and cooler service unit owned by the Columbus, Georgia bottler.

A 1950 Ford C.O.E. Model F6 operated by the San Antonio, Texas Coca-Cola Bottling Company.

A 1951 White, with Hobbs closed body, upon delivery to the San Antonio bottler.

A Los Angeles-based 1951 White Model 3015.

A 1952 White Model 3014 at an unknown location.

A 1952 White C.O.E. and driver ready to make deliveries.

A 1953 Dodge upon delivery to the Decatur, Alabama bottler.

A 1953 White Model 3015 during a delivery to a Cincinnati, Ohio supermarket.

1953 Ford C.O.E. Model P500 trucks.

A 1954 photograph of a North Carolina driver ready to roll.

A 1954 Ford F500 upon delivery to an Ohio bottler.

A 1955 Ford C.O.E. Model P500 photographed in front of the Louisville bottling company plant.

A 1955 Ford C.O.E. Model P350 ready for delivery to the Coca-Cola Bottling Company of Battle Creek, Michigan.

A 1955 Ford Model C600 pallet-type route truck at an unknown location.

A 1955 Chevrolet truck during a delivery to the Geelong Theatre.

A 1955 Ford Model C600 in service at Temple, Texas.

116

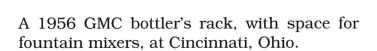

A 1956 GMC bottler's rack, with space for fountain mixers, at Cincinnati, Ohio.

A 1956 Chevrolet prior to delivery to the Atlanta Coca-Cola Bottling Company.

A 1957 International Model A-160 on a delivery run to an Atlanta shopping center.

A 1960 White C.O.E. delivering Coca-Cola to a Delta Airlines jet, Miami International Airport.

A 1962 International Loadstar at Chicago's Water Tower Inn.

A 1962 Chevrolet Nova wagon used for special promotions by the Danville, Virginia bottler.

1963 International Loadstar, upon delivery to the Fort Wayne works, and the 1937 International that it replaced.

A 1963 White Model 1500 Compact C.O.E. purchased by a Michigan bottler.

A 1964 Chevrolet ready for Atlanta deliveries.

A 1969 International Transtar C.O.E. Model CO-F407A sporting the new red and white paint scheme.